It's About Lincoln: More Snippets

Phil Gresham

Copyright © 2015 Philip A Gresham

All rights reserved.

ISBN:
ISBN-13: 978-1502946591

DEDICATION

This book is dedicated to my lovely wife for her continued support and unwavering patience as I continue to research the history of my home city.

PREFACE

This is the second book in the "It's About Lincoln: Snippets" series. The book is made up of a varied selection of stories about Lincoln, including: Joseph Ruston's "Bread and Cheese Hall", St Benedict's Church, Inns of Lincoln and the coming of the railway.

I hope you enjoy this book, you will find more information about Lincoln at http://www.itsaboutlincoln.co.uk. I can also be contacted via the "contact us" page on the website.

Phil Gresham

Lincoln

20th March 2015

Table of Contents

PREFACE vii

1 THE KING OF FRANCE SLEPT HERE? 1

2 IF YOU IGNORE ME I WILL IGNORE YOU 3

3 THIS FEE HAS NOTHING TO DO WITH SOLICITORS..................7

4 ARE INNS OUTT? 9

5 BREAD AND CHEESE HALL 11

6 BY MAIL COACH TO LONDON 13

7 A STAFFORDSHIRE MR DYKE BECAME MR WRIGHT IN LINCOLN 15

8 MORE INNS THAT ARE OUTT 17

9 ON THE WATER FRONT 19

10 ST KATHERINE'S PRIORY 23

11 LINCOLN'S CONNECTION WITH THOSE REBELLIOUS AMERICAN COLONISTS 27

12 THE CROSS ON THE CLIFF 29

13 PARDON ME BOY, IS THIS THE NOTTINGHAM CHOO CHOO..............31

14 "THE KING SMILED ..." 35

15 TRAGEDY ON PRINCESS STREET. 37

16 THE DECLINE AND RISE OF LINCOLN 41

17 BRITAIN'S GREATEST STREET 45

18 THE ELLISON'S OF BOULTHAM..49

19 WHERE THE VICARS' CHORAL ONCE LIVED 53

20 MR SHUTTLEWORTH AND HIS HALL 57

ABOUT THE AUTHOR 61

1 THE KING OF FRANCE SLEPT HERE?

The Dolphins was one of the oldest inns in Lincoln and stood at the corner of Eastgate and Priorygate. Alfred Shuttleworth purchased it in about 1892 and had it demolished as it spoilt his view of the Cathedral from his home, Eastgate House, now the Lincoln Hotel.

Here are the words of a notice that was displayed in the Dolphins:

"The sign of this Inn was the Minster Hostelry in the 14th century. The tenants of the Cathedral church, after paying their rents in the Common Chamber between the Minster and the Chapter House hard by were here entertained. As the rents were paid in corn and wool from the scarcity of coin, the landowners had large store house on the west side hereof leading to the Deanery. In the month of September in the year of our Lord 1356, the 28th year of the reign of King Edward III, his son Edward Prince of Wales commonly called the Black Prince from the colour of his armour, fought and won the battle of Poitiers in France, and took King John and his son the Dauphin prisoners. The Prince brought them to England, where they were put in the Charge of Saier de Rochford, the owner of Somerton Castle, near this city, who undertook to keep them for two shillings per day; a goodly sum when sheep were only 4d each. The following Easter Sir Saier de Rochford brought the King of France and the Dauphin to the Dean of this City, and after attending the Cathedral service they put up their horses and spent two days at this ancient inn, since which its sign has been The Dolphins."

It's a nice tale but is only loosely based on fact! Though the King of France, King John the Good, was held in captivity at **Somerton**

Castle from 4th August 1359 to 21st March 1360, the son the King had with him was Philip, his fourth son, the Dauphin remained in France after his father was captured. The King was placed under the protection of William, Baron d'Eyncoiurt; Sir Saier de Rochford was not the owner of Somerton Castle but one of the knights entrusted with keeping the Baron's captives. Furthermore, Easter was on 5th April 1360, King John was in London by this date.

Although the demolition of the Dolphin caused much distress among the people of Lincoln at the time, it is obvious that the north east view of the Cathedral was considerably improved. It also left room for the erection of Tennyson's statue in 1905.

Alfred Shuttleworth also purchased the building on the eastern corner of the Priorygate and Eastgate junction. The building was built in the late 17th century. The building was completely renovated and the exterior half timbered, becoming known as "Shuttleworth's Rest": people climbing Lindum Road could rest before continuing their journey.

2 IF YOU IGNORE ME I WILL IGNORE YOU

St Benedicts Church stands with its 'back' to the High Street on St Benedict's Square, almost saying "If you ignore me, I will ignore you". Lincolnians and visitors alike rush by the church giving

St Benedict's Church Today

little thought to this ancient building.

A Saxon church existed on the site at the time of the Norman conquest, although most of what we see today is of the 13th and 14th centuries. The church was once much grander and larger, a victim of the Civil War, the chancel and north aisle is all that remains. Many of Lincoln's churches were damaged or destroyed during the Civil War, only three churches were able to conduct public worship: St Peter at Arches, St Mary le Wigford and St Peter at Gowts.

The church was repaired after the Restoration and the tower was reconstructed against the west side of the medieval chancel arch, in a position to the east of the original tower.

The exterior gives little hint to the grandeur of the church prior to its partial demolition, at one time it was the church of the richest and most important people of the city. It was rebuilt at a time when Lincoln was in decline and no longer had the benefit of the Wool Staple.

In 1585 the Company of Barber Surgeons gifted a curfew bell to the church, hung in the bell tower. The bell was known as "Old Kate" and was later hung in the tower of St Marks, the bell returned to St Benedict's shortly before the demolition of St Mark's church in 1971

The story about "Old Kate" is from "Curiosities of the Belfry" by John Potter Briscoe.

"'Old Kate' was rung at 6 a.m. And 7 p.m. all year round. Old men say that (giving over work at seven in the evening) they used to listen for the welcome tones of 'Old Kate'. It was rung for many years by John Middlebrook, the parish clerk, who lived in a little lean-to tenement attached to the north side of the tower. On his death in December 1804, his wife succeeded him as parish clerk (her name was Mary Middlebrook; she was buried, as the Parish Register shows, on the 7th November 1822, being aged 72 years); and the story goes that the old lady consulted her conveninece and her duty at once by bringing the bell rope through the belfry door to her bedside, and pulled 'Old Kate' whilst she lay in bed. Afterwards old men, then boys, used to sleep in the widow's

tenement, (she being passed her work,) and they did the same, pulling the bell between them, "kneeling on the bed," and then lying down to sleep again. For this the Corporation paid 6s. 8d. a year down to 1837."

The parishioners of St Benedicts were transferred to the nearby St Peter at Arches church in 1783 when St Benedict's church was retired as a parish church. The City Corporation wanted to demolish the church in 1930 but it was saved by public subscription.

Today it is St Benedict's Centre and the Mothers Union will welcome you with "Rest & Refreshment" on a Tuesday, Thursday, Friday and Saturday between 10.00 a.m. and 2.30 p.m

3 THIS FEE HAS NOTHING TO DO WITH SOLICITORS

In the Middle Ages Lincoln was divided into districts, the City, the Close, the Bail. The Close and the Bail were self-governing, outside of the jurisdiction of the City. These areas were managed through local courts. The freemen made the laws and carried them out, the system was democratic as every freeman was expected to involve himself in the running of a district.

There was one other district in Lincoln that was outside of the jurisdiction of the City authorities during the middle ages. Prior to the Norman conquest there were a number of former Danelaw divisions of Lincoln that were ruled by the most powerful citizens. One of these divisions survived the conquest as a self-governing unit, the manor of Hungate.

The manor of Hungate was granted by Edward II to Henry de Beaumont. A manor house was built on the west side of the road now known as Beaumont Fee and to the south of West Parade. The house was known as Vesci Hall (Henry's sister, Isabella de Vesci, was granted the manor before Henry, she held it from about 1312 to 1335), the manor became known as "The Liberty of Beaumont Fee", and was the centre of the control of the Beaumont lands in the east of England. The definition of "fee" in this context is: an inherited or heritable estate in land

The Liberty of Beaumont Fee was held by the Beaumonts for about 200 years, but their lands were confiscated after the Wars of the Roses. In 1514 these lands were granted to Lord Howard, son of the Duke of Norfolk, for his support at the Battle of Flodden. The manor kept its independence until it was sold by the Norfolk family in 1700. It was then broken up between different owners and lost its privileges

Vesci Hall appears to have survived until the 1840s when John Hayward, the chemist, built Beaumont Manor on the site in the

Tudor Revival style, Lincoln corporation bought it in 1927. Currently used by UNISON as a social club.

Beaumont Manor today

4 ARE INNS OUTT?

The Inn has been a feature of English life for hundreds of years, providing sustenance to the traveller and a social place for local people. From the mid 17th century Coaching_Inns provided spare horses and food for travellers.

The movement of labour from the country to the town in the 19th century brought about a boom in housing with a corner shop on most streets and a pub not too far away. For over 100 years drinking at the 'local' pub was the most popular social activity for most adults, but the growth of other forms of entertainment have seriously affected the viability of many pubs. Lincoln has not been unaffected by this change, but I want to write about some of Lincoln's older inns.

The former Scarborough Arms

The Dolphin Inn (see "The King of France Slept Here" was erected in about the 14th century and was owned by the Dean and Chapter. The last licensee of the Dol-phin was Benjamin Arch who, at the 1891 census, was licensee at the Scar-borough Arms on Bailgate with his wife Sarah, his son, his widowed daughter and her son.

The Scarborough Arms stood at 21/22 Bailgate on the site of the Lloyds Bank building between Gordon Road and Westgate. The Scarborough Arms closed early in the 20th Century and the building was probably rebuilt at this time.

Charles E Roberts, hairdresser, had his shop there, at number 21, until at least 1942. Stanford & Sons, painters were at number 22 for a similar period.

Opposite The Scarborough Arms still stands The Lion & Snake, known as the "Ram", dating from the 15th century it then became the Lyon. In 1741 the "Snake" was added to the title in a lease granted to Clement Wood, Governor of the Castle. For a short time it became the Earl of Scarborough's Arms but by the late 18th century it became The Lion and Snake once more.

Where the White Hart Garage now stands was once the Swan Inn. The Swan closed in the late 18th Century and little is known about it. Opposite The Swan and next to the White Hart Hotel was The Angel.

The Angel was leased by the Dean and Chapter to Justice Robert Monson in 1580. Monson was Member of Parliament for Lincoln in 1563 and 1571, he became MP for Totnes in 1572. Part of the rent in the lease was "one cagg of fatt, sweet and good, wholesome sturgeon, with a jowl in it, which is to be presented yearly to the provost of the Cathedral on the Monday next before Holy Rood Day (14th September). In 1738 the Angel and the White Hart were both valued at £24, but by 1792 the latter was valued at £25 and the Angel only £10. Shortly after the Angel closed and was turned into residential accommodation.

5 BREAD AND CHEESE HALL

In 1889 Ruston, Proctor & Co's accountants certified that over the previous 7 years the company had made an average profit of £50,000 per year. The same year Joseph Ruston converted Ruston, Proctor & Company into a public company, for this he received £465,000 and he rewarded his most senior employees with shares to the value of £10,000.

The following year a demand was made by his workers for a pay rise, he refused the request with the reply:

"I hope you'll let me get bread and cheese out of my business!" After this Joseph Ruston was nicknamed 'Mr Bread and Cheese

The Drill Hall

In the same year he paid for a new Drill Hall for the First Lincoln Volunteer Company to be built at Broadgate, on the site of Newsums fire damaged woodyard. Inevitably the new building became known as 'Bread and Cheese Hall'. He could afford the cost as in 1890 the business made a profit of £96,000!

The Drill Hall was opened by Edward Stanhope, Secretary of State for War on 24th May 1890. The building was designed by Major F H Goddard of Goddard and Son, Lincoln. Built by H S & W Close of Lincoln of brick and Ancaster stone, with embattlements and watch tower, it provided a military aspect to its 55 ft frontage.

The gateway is 10 ft wide with the Royal Arms carved out of stone above. On the right was the officers' room with an apartment 24 ft by 18 ft, to the left was the Adjutant's room of the same dimensions with an office for the Sergeant Major. The hall beyond was 140 ft long by 50 ft wide. The floor of the hall was specially constructed to deaden the noise of drilling men, made of blocks 10in by 2.5 in by 1.5 in, laid in pitch on a solid concrete foundation.

There was also a soup kitchen with coppers and appliances of every type for use at times of need, no doubt it came in useful when used for the smallpox epidemic of 1904/5.

Above the hall was a balcony for 150 people and a recreation room.

There was an armoury of sufficient size to store the arms of the whole battalion. On the north side of the hall was a 50 ft by 50 ft gymasium.

It had been suggested that Ruston knew that to give his employees an increase in wages to his employees would probably put other local engineering companies out of business! But is that too kind to an entrepreneur who was well known for his hard business head and tough negotiating style?

6 BY MAIL COACH TO LONDON

Before the arrival of the railways getting from point a to point b wasn't easy. Walking was probably the most common form of travel for most people, travelling by horse was for those who could afford it but the more fortunate would travel by Mail Coach.

The Mail Coach came into being in the late 18th century. The period from 1810 to 1830 was the "Golden Age" of coach travel, road surfaces had improved and coaches could attain average speeds of 12 mph.

The "Royal Mail" coach that operated from the Saracen's Head and the Reindeer

This is a record of the Journey by mail coach from Lincoln to London, before the arrival of the railway:

"Leaving Lincoln by the mail at 2 p.m., supping at Peterborough at 9, the traveller, after composing himself for an uneasy slumber about Yaxley Barracks (from whence the waters of Whittlesea Mere might be seen shimmering in the moonlight), grumbling through a weary night at the obstinate legs of his opposite neighbour, and sorely pinched in the small of the back, was only delivered, cold and cross, at the Spre(a)d Eagle, Gracechurch Street, about 5 the next morning. He had then the choice of going to bed, with feet like ice, in a fireless room, opening out on an open-air gallery (where a box was fixed for the barber to shave travellers), or of sulking in a fusty coffee-room till the waiters were astir and the world was aired." - The Lincoln Pocket Guide, Sir Charles H J Anderson.

Fifteen hours to London may seem slow to us today but in the 1840s it must have been quite rapid. People made their wills before they were "received into the York stage-coach, which performed the journey to London (if God permitted) in four days."

In 1786 the cost of a coach from Lincoln to London via Newark, Grantham, Stamford, etc. was £1 11s 6d (£1.58) for inside passengers and 15s 9d (£0.79) for the less fortunate on the outside. To put the price into perspective, in 1797 an agricultural labourer earned £30.03 per annum and surgeons £174.95 per annum.

Mail coaches continued into the 1840s but the arrival about this time of the railways spelled the end of this "romantic" form of travel.

7 A STAFFORDSHIRE MR DYKE BECAME MR WRIGHT IN LINCOLN

Albert George Dyke was born in 1863 at Penkridge, Staffordshire, his parents were William and Hester Dyke. In the 1881 census William's, occupation was listed as "Ale Merchant", living in Penkridge. Prior to this (1869-1880) he was licensee/owner of the George & Fox at Penkridge. The move to Lincoln later in the 1880s was due to William's financial difficulties and possibly the reason why Albert didn't call his new business "A G Dyke".

In the 1891 census Albert and his parents were living at 16 Orchard Street, Lincoln. William's occupation was now shown as "Corn Merchants Labourer" and Albert was a "Confectioner (Em'ee)".

Albert established R M Wright in the early 1890s. Albert's sister, Sarah, married Richard Merry Wright in 1877, so that explains where the name R M Wright came from .

Albert married Rose Emma Horner in 1894. Between 1895 and 1902 they had 3 children, the last was Ralph Montague Wright Dyke, named obviously with intention of taking over the business later, sadly Ralph died in 1903.

In 1901 Census Albert and Rose were living at 88 Bailgate, Lincoln, Cycle & Motor Manufacturers Agent. By 1911 they were living close to the business at 12 Newland.

He was a keen motorist involved with motoring clubs in Lincoln and Nottingham, this led to the early success of his business: he entered competitions in the name of R M

Wright to give publicity to his business. To prove the reliability of the Humber car he organised a 5,000 mile trial.

He re-formed the business as R M Wright & Co Ltd before 1919. They were agents for many makes of heavy commercial vehicles , farm tractors and Ford dealers. There was a hire department with a fleet of taxicabs and private-hire cars Albert liquidated the company in 1927 shortly after the death of his wife. A New company, R M Wright (1927) Ltd was formed.

In 1932 Albert lived at 50 Nettleham Road. He died in Oswestry in 1940.

By the 1950s Wrights were main distributors for Austin motor vehicles, continuing through British Motor Corporation the nationalised British Leyland Motor Holdings, British Leyland and the Rover Group Unfortunately, financial health of the company was closely linked to that of its supplier. It was obvious to the owners of the company, Lincolnshire Co-operative Limited, that the Rover Group was in trouble so it was decided that R M Wright, after over 100 years of trading, would be wound up and the Lincoln premises would be re-branded as Holland Bros and the more appealing Jaguar products would be retailed.

In early 2012 Lincolnshire Co-operative Ltd sold Holland Bros to the Marshall Motor Group.

8 MORE INNS THAT ARE OUTT

The George Inn was a large wooden building on the corner of Guildhall Street where HSBC Bank now stands. The Corporation rebuilt it in 1741 "with brick and stone in a grand manner" and "cost the City upwards of £2,000", it was renamed the **Reindeer and** later it became the **City Arms**.

It was not uncommon for such a place as this to have a cockpit. When James I visited Lincoln in March 1617 he watched a cockfight at the George. He had four cocks put in the pit together and "the resulting uproar gave him huge delight".

The King then crossed the road to the **Spread Eagle** where there was a fencing match between a fencer of the city and an attendant of the court in which the Lincoln man had the best of it. "The King then called for his porter, who took the sword and buckler and gave and received a broken pate."

The Spread Eagle was one of Lincoln's principal coaching inns in the 18th and 19th century and many political meetings were held here. In common with many such places it had its own brew house. There was an archway in the High Street frontage for mail coaches to enter the yard where there were extensive stables. The Spread Eagle closed in 1923 and was sold to the F W Woolworth chain of stores.

Near the Stonebow was **The Saracens Head**, a coaching inn that closed in 1959. In 1600 two priests were staying there, one of them, Thomas Hurt, had escaped from Wisbech

Castle. They were brought before the Mayor who sent them on to the Assize where they were convicted as "Seminary Priests" and sentenced to death by Judge Glandvil. They were hanged, drawn and quartered on Canwick Hill.

In the 18th century Lincoln's theatre was on Drury Lane, in the late 18th century the theatre moved* downhill to the **King's Arms Inn** on the High Street. A new theatre, The Theatre Royal, opened here in 1806. The King's Arms closed in the 1830s. The yard of the same name survives to this day.

* Some sources suggest that the theatre moved to its new site at King's Arms Yard in 1763 but there was a performance of the play "Country Girl" at the Drury Lane Theatre Royal on December 16th 1774

9 ON THE WATER FRONT

The area of Lincoln bordered by Waterside North, Broadgate and Monks Road in the last half of the 19th century had a rapid growth of population. The houses in the south of the area close to Waterside South were generally of poor quality and most were demolished during the slum clearances of the 1930s.

The reason for this expansion of housing was two-fold:

> By 1861 Clayton, Shuttleworth & Company was employing 900 men at their works on Waterside South, Ruston, Proctor & Co was also there and by 1881 they had 1,000 employees. Over the years more businesses made their base close to the Waterside/Stamp End area, including Richard Duckering's Foundry.
>
> The population of Lincoln had soared from 7,200 in 1801 to almost 21,000 in 1861.* Over the same period the population of the parish of St Swithin's, which covered a large part of the Stamp End/Waterside area, grew from 940 to 4,655. By 1901 St Swithin's parish, Cold Bath House and the new Monks Liberty population had grown to 10,356: **the population of England in 1801 was 8,308,000 and 1861 was 18,776,300, an increase of 126%, whereas Lincoln's grew by almost 200%!**

> In 1869 The Corporation of the City of Lincoln, recognising the lack of suitable housing for the increased population, Applied to Parliament for the Lincoln City Commons Act to be passed. The purpose of this Act was as follows:

"Improvement of Streets, Compulsory Purchase of Lands, Purchase by Corporation of Common Rights over Monks' Leys Common, Power to Corporation to Borrow on Borough Fund and on West Common, Sale of Commons, Power to Lease Commons and Common Rights, Improvement of West and South Commons, Establishment of Public Park, Maintenance thereof out of Borough Fund, Application of Purchase Moneys for and of Rents of Commons, Annuities to Freemen, Bye-laws, Regulation of Common Rights, Exchange of Lands, Incorporation and Amendment of Acts, and other purposes. " The main effects of this on the area covered in this post was to allow the widening of Monks' Lane (later re-named Monks' Road), the using of Monks Leys Common for building and permission to borrow money to complete these and other undertakings. This meant that a large area of what is now known as "green-belt" land was available for building on.

From 1870 until well into the Edwardian age extensive house building took place in most parts of Lincoln, but mainly in the Monks' Road area, the High Street Canwick Road area and St Catherines. In the Monks Road area housing was built for all levels of society: the foundry and factory workers lived mainly on the roads leading off Monks Road and the more well-to-do lived on Monks' Road near to Broadgate or above the former Monks Leys Common on Lindum Terrace.

JTB Porter & Co in 1878 fabricated Cottingham's Bridge at their Gowts Bridge Works and erected it over the River Witham at Waterside North so that the workers living in the Stamp End could easily reach their place of work at

Waterside South. The bridge was paid for by public

Cottingham's Bridge

subscription, initiated by the Mayor, William Cottingham.

A large part of Monks' Leys Common was used for public recreation with the opening of the Arboretum in 1872. This was the age of public parks when it became increasingly recognised that places for the public to perambulate and promenade were essential for improving the well-being of the individual.

Throughout England there was movement of labour from the country to the towns and cities, but in many newly industrialised towns labour moved in from all parts of Great Britain. In Lincoln workers were drawn here by Ruston, Proctor & Co, Clayton, Shuttleworth & Co., William Foster, Charles Duckering Ltd and other growing industrial concerns.

The hundred years from 1850 saw the revival of Lincoln's fortunes but by the 1970s all but one of the above companies had been taken over, moved away or closed down: The sole survivor is Ruston, Proctor & Co which, through its many changes of ownership and name became Siemens. Siemens have consolidated their position in Lincoln as its major employer with their recent move to Teal Park of its HQ and service department.

10 ST KATHERINE'S PRIORY

St Katherine's Priory, across the Sincil Drain from the Great Bargate, was established by Bishop de Chesney in 1148 as a Gilbertine house. The Gilbertines, founded by St Gilbert of Sempringham, were the only Lincolnshire religious order and the only order that allowed men and

Postern Gate on Greestone Stairs

women to join as secular and lay members.

The Priory offered hospitality to its visitors, not only church dignitaries but also royalty and the nobility stayed here before entering the city. In 1181 Hugh of Avalon stayed with the prior before proceeding barefoot to his enthronement in the Cathedral. The route of his procession is not known but he no doubt followed the Roman Ermine Street along the High Street and Greestone Stairs, entering the Cathedral via the south eastern porch. Successive bishops did the same, the streets were draped with cloth, which was then distributed to the poor, the tradition continued until 1530 when the Cathedral broke with Rome .

When Bishop Hugh of Avalon, later St Hugh, died in 1199 in London his body was brought to St Katherine's before being taken to the Cathedral in a procession led by King John. Bishop Hugh was Canonized on 17 February 1220 by Pope Honorius III.

The most famous visitors to St Katherine's Priory were Edward I and the body of his Queen, Eleanor.

Queen Eleanor was taken ill while at Clipstone Castle, Nottinghamshire, where her husband Edward I was holding parliament. They left Clipstone to journey to Lincoln, Eleanor's condition worsened as they reached Harby. The journey was halted and the queen was lodged at the home of Sir Richard de Weston, a knight of her train. Medical aid was summoned from Lincoln and after two months she passed away, on 29th November 1290 aged 49.

Edward was heartbroken and decreed that her body should be embalmed and taken to London. The body was embalmed at St Katherine's Priory. Eleanor's body rested at the Priory for five days.

Her viscera was placed in a magnificent altar-tomb in Lincoln Cathedral, with an effigy in gilt copper, under the east window, but it was destroyed in 1644 during the Civil War. Joseph Ruston bore the cost of the restoration or the tomb.

The first of the "Eleanor Crosses" was erected at Swine Green south of St Catherine's and the Royal train began its 11 day journey to London, a cross was erected at each of the nights' stops. Eleanor's funeral took place in Westminster Abbey on 17 December 1290.

11 LINCOLN'S CONNECTION WITH THOSE REBELLIOUS AMERICAN COLONISTS

The regiment that was known until 1960 as the Lincolnshire Regiment was formed in 1685 as The Earl of Bath's Regiment, in 1751 it was renamed the 10th Regiment of Foot.

In 1767 the Regiment sailed to the British Colonies in America. While they were there the "Boston Tea Party", otherwise known as "The Destruction of the Tea", occurred, as a protest over the Tea Tax instituted by the British Government in London.

The escalation of the crisis resulted in the start of the American Revolutionary War on 19th April 1775 near Boston with the Battle of Lexington and Concord. The British forces suffered a defeat and marched to Bunker and Breeds Hills to prevent the colonists from bombarding Boston from Breeds Hill which stands on a peninsular overlooking the City. Although it was seen as a victory for the British armies, their numbers of killed and wounded were far higher than those of the colonists, of which officer casualties were disproportionately high.

The result was seen as a victory at home and to commemorate it a hill on Wragby Road, Lincoln, was named Bunker's Hill, in honour of the Lincolnshire forces that fought at the battle - a name it retains to this day.

The 10th had the name "North Lincolnshire Regiment" added in 1782, in 1881 it was renamed as the "Lincolnshire Regiment" and in 1946 became the "Royal Lincolnshire

Regiment". Following a series of amalgamations the regiment became the "Second Battalion The Royal Anglian Regiment 'The Poacher's " in 1992.

The Cathedral from Bunker's Hill

Incidentally, the term "Yeller-Belly" is said to come from the yellow waistcoats of the 10th Regiment of Foot, there are also other explanations.

12 THE CROSS ON THE CLIFF

The first of the twelve Eleanor Cross's stood at the junction of High Street, South Park and St Catherines, not far from the present St Catherine's Priory Centre and the foot of Cross o' Cliff Hill. At the top of the hill stood another cross, this cross marked the boundary of the southern limits of the City of Lincoln. By 1600 this cross had been removed "by some evil-disposed person". The Corporation ordered that a stone should be erected in its place as a landmark.

It was at this spot that the dignitaries of the Corporation met distinguished visitors arriving from the South. In 1445, the Mayor, the Sheriffs and aldermen, on bended knees, here received Henry VI and his young bride, Margaret of Anjou.

Here 172 years later, on March 17th, 1617, the civic authorities all "in long cloth clothes of purple in grain", the Sheriffs with white staves of office, the others carrying javelins fringed with red and white, waited to meet James I, who had been hunting along the Heath on his way from Grantham; it appears that the king took a different route and missed the civic party.

In 1844 a rural walk, known as the Promenade, was created along the upper part of the Common, the Common was enclosed by iron railings at about the same time. The walk was landscaped by turning former quarrying works into a terrace, parts of which still remain, and the planting of trees

The Cathedral from the Promenade

13 PARDON ME BOY, IS THIS THE NOTTINGHAM CHOO CHOO

Lincoln was one of the last major towns or cities to be linked by rail, a line from London to Cambridge had been proposed in 1825 and would have extended to York via Lincoln, this route was abandoned. In the event, the London to York line followed a route to the west of the River Trent mainly due to the lobbying of Doncaster's MP, who believed that a line running through Lincoln would be detrimental to his town.

Railway promoters became active again in 1833 when three routes were proposed through Lincoln. In March 1835 a Lincoln committee under the chairmanship of Thomas Norton, the City's mayor, reported on the alternative routes. Again, nothing came of this move to bring the railway to Lincoln.

In 1845 a meeting of 6,000 people at the Beast Market, next to the Sessions House, ended in a free fight when the chairman, the Lincoln mayor announced that the London to York line had won the right to serve Lincoln. Opponents claimed that labourers had been brought at 2/- a piece to vote for the London to York project. George Hudson, "The Railway King", had spent a lot of money opposing the line in favour of his Midland Railway. His boast was that he would bring a railway to Lincolnshire while the rest were still talking about it!

Hudson's boast came true when the Midland Railway brought the first route into Lincoln from Nottingham. The line opened on 3rd August 1846, the first train left Nottingham at 9 am, stopping off at the various villages en route to pick up those invited to celebrate the new enterprise, and arriving at Lincoln at 11 am.

It was an important day for the city: the buildings and streets were decorated, the bells of the Cathedral and churches ringing peals at intervals, the band of the 4th Irish Dragoons played the "Railway Waltz" as two trains left the Midland Station, carrying local dignitaries and cannon were fired. The journey to Nottingham took almost 2 hours. The return journey was in heavy rain. A banquet was held in the National School in Silver Street.

Unfortunately there was a casualty of all the merriment: a man called Paul Harden has his leg shattered by the bursting of a cannon in the station yard. He was taken to the County Hospital where his leg was amputated.

The Great Northern Railway opened in 1848, this line was routed from Peterborough through rural Lincolnsire, via Sleaford. Lincoln now had two railways crossing the High Street. The town clerk was sent to London to enquire whether both lines could be routed through one crossing, but he was assured that the crossings would not have a detrimental affect on the flow of the road traffic using the

The Elegant Portico of St Mark's Station

High Street.

The coming of the railways completely transformed Lincoln's communications with other parts of the country. The produce of Lincolnshire's farms and factories could be easily transported and in return coal for homes and industry could be brought into the county. Travelling by mail coach to London took 13 hours whereas by train it would take a mere 4 hours: a businessman could leave Lincoln early in the morning transact his business in London and return home in the evening to sleep in his own bed.

In less than 5 years railway lines radiated from Lincoln in all directions.

Prince Albert passed through Lincoln in 1849 to lay the

foundation stone of the Grimsby docks. On the 27th August 1851 Queen Victoria, Prince Albert and the Prince of Wales had a brief stop at Lincoln, en route for Balmoral. An address was read by the Mayor and he presented the keys of the city, following Her Majesty's reply some grapes that had been grown by Richard Ellison of Sudbrooke Holm were also presented. The Prince of Wales, later King Edward VII, was a regular visitor to the city by train, mainly for the horse racing, as a guest of Henry Chaplin of Blankney Hall.

The Midland Station, otherwise known as St Mark's Station, closed 11 May 1985, the Great Northern Station, now known as the Central Station continues to operate from St Mary's Street.

14 "THE KING SMILED ..."

William III and Queen Mary II visited the Lincoln in the 1690s*

"... having visited Lincoln, while on their tour through the Kingdom, (the King) made the citizens an offer to serve them in any manner they liked best. They asked for a Fair, though it was harvest, when few people can attend it, and though the town had no trade nor any manufacture. The King smiled, and granted their request; observing it was a humble one indeed."

The fair was held in Broadgate on the first Wednesday after the 12th September, lasting until the Friday. This fair became known as the "Fools' Fair" as most of the potential buyers would be busy with harvest, but it was recorded in 1787 as the largest show of cattle in Lincoln for many years.

Other sales of animals were held in this area at the Beast Market, near the Clask Gate and Monks Lane, the Pig Market (now Unity Square) on the east side of Broadgate and Sheep Market on the site of the present St Swithin's Church.

Broadgate follows the line of the Roman and medieval lower city defences and is built outside the city walls, on top of the filled in ditch. It was common practice to build outside city walls as the land inside was too valuable to build wide roads. Broadgate was not a major Lincoln thoroughfare until the new Thorn Bridge was built in the early 19th century.

The increase in traffic meant that the fair was causing an obstruction so it was moved to the new Cattle Market on Monks Road in 1846.

Today, Broadgate is probably the busiest road in Lincoln, the north and south bound traffic being separated by a central reservation. The northbound traffic has an excellent view of Lincoln Cathedral perched 200 ft above.

The year I found during my research was 1696 and that William viited with his queen, but Mary died of smallpox in 1694.

15 TRAGEDY ON PRINCESS STREET.

This news item was published on August 26th, 1911. Additional information is added at the end:

Fireman killed by falling wall

AN outbreak of fire that illuminated the whole city between 11 pm and midnight on Wednesday (23rd August) *promptly called to the minds of those who saw the distant flames the riots* of Friday and Saturday and the terrorising of peaceful citizens.*

Unhappily, there is a loss of life to report, one of the best known firemen in the Brigade being sacrificed to the call of duty. A well-known tradesman of the city died from his injuries at 4 pm on Friday.

Nor was this all the sad side of the story.

There was a great crowd looking on from across the river amongst whom were numbers who hooted loudly at the hardworking Brigade and cheered when shortage of water compelled the motor fire engine to slow down. What was infinitely worse, half bricks and stones were flung at a constable who was struggling in three feet of mud to get the hose into deeper water of the Witham. The scene of the blaze was Messrs Osborne's motor works, near the bottom of Princess Street. Adjoining it is Messrs Pennell's seed warehouse, which stands on the edge of the Witham.

At 11.20pm a telephone message for the fire engine was received from Messrs Ruston, Proctor and Co.'s wood works to the effect that Le Tall's Mill was on fire.

The motor fire engine was quickly got away in charge of the Captain (Chief Constable Coleman).

At 11.25pm the roof had gone and a gigantic sheet of flame was leaping to the sky, silhouetting the mill tower.

People, many aroused from their slumbers by the discharge of a bomb as a signal for the Waterworks to put on the pressure, were running towards the scene from all parts of the city.

The street in which the works are situated is one of the oldest and narrowest in Lincoln, and it was a good thing that a strong body of county police, under Inspector Wild, were promptly on the spot, and drew a cordon across the top of Salthouse Lane, which opens into Princess Street. The motor fire engine was taken to the bottom of Princess Street, and a connection made with the river, but from the first the difficulty of obtaining water was apparent.

The flames were now, of course, consuming everything within the four-storey building. Blazing beams were crashing to the ground and metal work was twisted and wrenched into the most grotesque shapes.

It is an old water main that runs down this side street and it is wholly inadequate for a big fire. Another difficulty occurred when a stand pipe broke.

Eventually the hose was attached to the main water pipe in High Street and powerful pressure obtained. Even then the handicaps were not done with, for at the terrific pace the motor was now working the lengths of hose burst in several places and many of the firemen were drenched to the skin, as were spectators. As section after section showed considerable bursts, the water had to be eventually shut off until repairs were made.

There was not less than 900 feet of hose paid out to High Street. Several jets were directed into the premises and the men got the flames well under in a few minutes, with the exception of odd corners.

It was after the fire was got well down that the fatality occurred. The crash of the falling wall could be heard some distance away. This was about 1am. As quickly as possible the two men were extricated from the debris, and Clay was carried into the house of Mr Thomas Brown, 25 Princess Street, where he expired almost immediately.

Versions differ as to whether Fireman Clay had mounted a ladder and was directing his jet into the building from the height of the first floor, with Mr T. H. Starmer holding the foot of the ladder, or whether the two of them were on the ground level.

What is certain is that a large portion of the tall brick wall at the back of the premises collapsed upon them both, entombing the fireman. Mr Starmer was also very seriously injured, the chief hurt being a fractured skull, and he was removed on the horse ambulance to the County Hospital, where death took place yesterday afternoon.

Messrs Osborne, who have occupied the premises about five years, estimate their loss at about £1,000, which is only partly covered by insurance.

The smouldering remnants of the interior of the motor works assumed a sufficiently threatening aspect about noon on Thursday as to warrant the fire engine again being despatched, under Engineer Vessey, and for almost three quarters of an hour all parts of the building were played upon with the hose, until the remotest aspect of danger was removed.

Police Constable Clay was one of the most cheery and popular members of the Force. He was a native of North Wheatley, Nottinghamshire, where he was born on April 18th, 1873. He came to Lincoln as a farm labourer, joined the Force on June 1st, 1892, so that he had very nearly 20 years' service to his credit.

At this time the fire service was manned by police officers, a separate 'Fire Brigade' was created under the Fire Brigades Act 1938

A glowing account of P C Clay was written in the article but very little about Mr Starmer: Thomas Henry Starmer was born in Lincoln in 1862 and married Emma Millns in 1886, together they operated a picture framing business on nearby Scorer Street. It is likely he saw the fire from his home and went over to help.

As far as I can see Osbornes' business didn't survive the fire but Mrs Starmer occupied the workshop in 1913 continuing the picture framing business, did she get the workshop as compensation?

Emma Starmer died in 1927

* The Lincoln riots have been written about in Pat Nurses book "Devils Let Loose"

16 THE DECLINE AND RISE OF LINCOLN

Lincoln is one of nine cities and nine towns in England that were given the status "County of the City of ...", such places are called County Corporate.

Counties Corporate were created during the Middle Ages, and were effectively small self-governing counties of no prescribed size but usually including some surrounding countryside and villages. They usually covered towns or cities which were deemed to be important enough to be independent from their county. Each town or city's charter was drafted according to its needs, in some cases there was a security issue which brought about the status, i.e. Poole was plagued by pirates so became County of the Town of Poole.

While they were administratively distinct counties, with their own sheriffs, most of the counties corporate remained part of the "county at large" for purposes such as the county assize courts. From the 17th century the separate jurisdictions of the counties corporate were increasingly merged with that of the surrounding county, so that by the late 19th century the title was mostly a ceremonial one.

Lincoln's County Corporate status was made by a Royal Charter dated 21st November 1409. The main points of the charter were:

- The election of two sheriffs instead of bailiffs.

- The city to be called the County and City of Lincoln.

- The Mayor to be the King's Escheator[1].

- The power to render accounts to the King's Exchequer by attorney.

- The Mayor and Sheriffs with four others to be justices of the peace, with defined jurisdiction.

- A yearly fair beginning fifteen days before the feast of the deposition of St. Hugh (17 November) and continuing for fifteen days after.

- The receipt in aid of the payment of the city rent of 180*l*. of the annual rent of 6*l*. paid to the Crown by the weavers of Lincoln; strictly and fully reserving the exemption from the jurisdiction of the city of the cathedral church, the Close, and the Dean and Chapter.

The Charter was witnessed at Westminster by the archbishops of Canterbury and York, the bishops of London, Durham, and Bath and Wells, Edward duke of York, John earl of Somerset, chamberlain, John Typtot, treasurer, master John Prophete keeper of the Privy Seal, and John Stanley, steward of the household..

By the 15th century Lincoln's fortunes were on the wane, it's Jewish community, the second largest in he country after London, had been expelled 100 years before and in 1369 the <u>Staple</u>[2] was moved to Boston: the population of Lincoln had fallen to its lowest level because of these reasons and the Black Death which ravaged most of England at this time. Buildings were demolished and the land was turned back to farming, even within the city walls.

Lincoln's population at this time was in the region of about 2,000, drastically down from its 6,000 at the time of the Conquest. Many churches were closed, some were demolished, there being parishes that were uninhabited.

Lincoln started to revive in the 18th century due to many factors, the main one being Richard Ellisons leasing and making navigable again the Fosdyke. The population grew and at the 1801 census there were over 7,200 people in Lincoln, but by 1901 the population had grown to nearly 49,000. The Industrial Revolution had arrived!

In 1466 a Charter was granted by Edward IV "to the Mayor Thomas Grantham and the citizens, in relief of the desolation and ruin which had come upon the city, that the villages of Braunstone, Wadyugtone, Bracebrigge and Canwik should be separated from the county and annexed to the county of the city, with the transfer of all jurisdiction of sheriffs etc., that all their inhabitants should contribute to scot and lot and all the charges of the city, and none be allowed to dwell within the liberties of the city who should refuse so to do... "

County Corporates were abolished through Government Acts in the 19th century, notably the Militia Act 1882 and Local Government Act 1888, Lincoln becoming part of Lncolnshire Coiunty Council but retaining it's City Council status.

The list of Counties Corporate and when created

1. County of the City of ...
- Canterbury (1471)
- Coventry (1451, abolished 1842)

- Exeter (1537)
- Lichfield (1556)
- Lincoln (1409)
- London (1132 until 1965)
- Norwich (1404)
- Worcestor (1622)
- York (1396)

2. County of the Town of
- Bristol (1373, City since 1542)
- Chester (1238/1239, City since 1541)
- Gloucester (1483, City since 1541)
- Newcastle upon Tyne (1400)
- Nottingham (1448)
- Poole (1571)
- Southampton (1447)

3. Borough and Town of ...
- Berwick upon Tweed (1551)
- 4. Kingston upon Hull became County of Hullshire by charter of 1440, restricted to Town and County Kingston upon Hull in 1835

1. Person appointed to receive property of a person who died intestate.

2. Lincoln was originally granted the Wool Staple in 1313 due to the importance of its Cloth industry, its loss was a blow that Lincoln didn't recover from for a very long time.

17 BRITAIN'S GREATEST STREET

Lincoln's Steep Hill says it as it is, it's steep.

Leading from Castle Hill it drops the best part of 200 feet, following the route of the Roman Ermine Street, to the top of the High Street, via the Strait.

Walking down Steep Hill the first historical item you meet is a stone in the wall on the left, the only visible remains of the south gate of the upper part of Lindum Colonia. Parts of this gate were standing in 1788 when Gough visited the city, but the arch was demolished in the early 1700s by a householder on the east side of the gate. Those that were employed to demolish it used a heavy beam battering ram style to knock out the crown stone expecting the rest of the arch to collapse, but it didn't they had to knock out each stone

Just a few steps down on the left is Norman House. Once known as "Aaron the Jews

House", but Aaron is known to have lived either in the Bail, above here., or in a house where Harding House now stands
The Norman House is a 12th-century stone building originally with shops on the ground floor and domestic rooms above. It has had a lot of rebuilding over the centuries but traces remain of the front chimney stack, ornamental string-course and doorway. The building is now home to a bag shop and a tea retailer

Below the Norman House is an open area where five roads meet, this was once the site of the fish market.

The first building on the right of Steep Hill is The Harlequin, a beautiful half timbered building adding to the charm of Steep Hill. The Harlequin opened it's doors as an inn in 1744 and closed in the 1920s, it is now a secondhand bookshop.

From here the hill becomes much steeper, on the right are more quaint shops selling a variety of things. On the left stands Harding House, a 15th century building, named after Canon Harding who bought it in the 1930s to save it from demolition. On the ground floor are items for sale by local artists and upstairs is a gallery area where works of local artists are exhibited.

The road turns left below here into Danesgate, but Steep Hill continues as a pedestrian only route. At the top of this the steeped part of the hill is The Mayors Chair, said to have been originally placed by a mayor of Lincoln in 1732 to give the weary traveller a chance to rest before ascending the rest of Steep Hill. The original chair has been replaced by a chair made by local artist Richard Bett, the new chair fits well into its surroundings.

The railings behind the Mayors Chair were first erected in the early 18th century to prevent carriages and carts negotiating this very steep part of the hill. There is a tale that Charles de Laet Waldo Sibthorp drove a "four in hand" all the way down Steep Hill, but I doubt it's validity, the railings were erected almost 100 years before he was born.

At the bottom of this part of the hill 9 Steep Hill, a former decorators shop which still displays the name of "E Haigh" in gold leaf on glass.

On the left of Steep Hill, almost opposite E Haigh's shop is Well Lane. The Romans would use this easier gradient to get their horse-drawn vehicles up the hill to the Colonia.

E Haigh's former shop

At the corner of Well Lane is a Grade II listed mid-19th century water pump in a tapered square case.

On the right almost at the bottom of Steep Hill are Jews Court and Jews House.

Jews Court, is a 17th & 18th century building, it is thought that it was once the site of a Jewish synagogue, but this may have been to the rear of Jews House. Jews Court is the home of the Society for Lincolnshire History and Archaeology.

Jews House

Jews Court

Jews House is one of the most important 12th century stone houses in Britain. It has a rich ornamental doorway and chimney. The building originally consisted of a hall at first floor level above thr shop and storage spaces at ground level.. Although much changed over the years some original features remain: The elaborately carved doorways and romanesque windows. When the Jews were expelled from England in 1290, the owner was Belaset daughter of Solomon of Wallingford.

Steep Hill is separated here from the High Street by a short stretch of road called 'Strait'.

Steep Hill was given Britain's Greatest Street Award by the Academy of Urbanism in 2012.

18 THE ELLISON'S OF BOULTHAM

Boultham Park was bought by Richard Ellison for his illegitimate son Colonel Richard Ellison sometime before his death in 1827. Col Ellison married Charlotte Chetwynd of Staffordshire in 1830.

The hall was built in the mid 1840s and the grounds were laid out. The park was formerly part of the village of Boultham, the villagers were displaced to make way for the park

A large ornamental lake was dug in 1857 and some Roman remains were found. The hall was re-modelled and enlarged in 1874, using designs drawn up by William Watkins.

The bird bath shown in the adjoining picture is now in the graveyard of St Helen's Church.

Col Ellison erected a large monument, in the design of an urn, to Simon, his favourite horse, the monument now stands nearby in Simon's Green.

Simon's Memorial

Following Col Ellison's death in 1881, Boultham Hall passed to Lt Colonel

Richard George Ellison. Lt Col Ellison had a distinguished military career, during the Crimean War he fought at Alma, Inkerman, Sebastol and the capture of Balaclava. On his return to Lincoln he was met at the railway station by the Mayor and Corporation, who took him in an open carriage with 4 horses to Boultham, where they lunched, and "half the town had cheese and ale"

Boultham Hall had extensive grounds: what is now Boultham Park Road was a private road which lead to another private road north of, and parallel to Dixon Street and joined the road to a gatehouse on the High Street.

High Street gatehouse to Boultham Hall

Lt Colonel Ellison was the last resident of the hall. On his death in 1908 it passed to Richard Todd Ellison who sold the Hall and grounds in 1913 to a Nottingham company. The contents of the Hall were auctioned over 5 days in 1913.

During the First World War, the house served as a convalescence home for soldiers.

After the war much of the land was sold for new housing. On 15 May 1929 Lincoln Corporation purchased the Hall and remaining grounds from J A MacDonald and D E Smith, Nottingham-based developers, for £6,000 for the creation of a public park.

During World War Two, areas of the park were planted with sugar beet as part of the Dig for Victory campaign.

The grounds were laid out as a public park and the hall was demolished in 1959. The only remaining evidence of the hall is a plinth and steps.

The Plinth is in the background of this photo

Boultham Park is one of the many green spaces within the boundary of the City of Lincoln, and has been enjoyed by thousands of local people since 1929.

19 WHERE THE VICARS' CHORAL ONCE LIVED

In the medieval period Lincoln was divided into three areas: the City, the Bail and the Close; each was a locally independent self-governing place. The Close was, and still is the area surrounding the Cathedral, housing the priests and officials of the Cathedral, together with their servants and those involved in the operation of the Cathedral and the Close. It is believed that the Close came into being at the time of the building of the Cathedral.

This was the wealthiest area of Lincoln in the 12th century encouraging "cutpurses", thieves and murderers to frequent the area at night preying on the people of the Close.

The Dean and Chapter (under the instruction of Oliver, bishop of Lincoln) were granted licenses to crenellate the Close, "for their (the clergy) better safety from night attacks in passing from their houses to the said church". The first licence was issued on 8th May 1285 for a 12 foot wall (the licence was repeated in 1316) the second was issued in 1318 to raise the wall and add turrets. The main entrance to the Close was Exchequergate, all the gates were double, with a courtyard between the sets of gates, except for Pottergate and Greestone gate, where the incline precluded use of two gates. The licences required the gates to be open during the day.

The boundary wall of the Close was intact in 1722 with three of four towers, and is still standing in many places.

The Number Houses

It is thought that the first Lincoln houses to have numbers were in the Close, the "Number Houses", built after the mid 18th century and somewhat modernised and altered since.

There are over 80 buildings in the Close, most of which are in the ownership of the Cathedral, many of the buildings are of Grade 1, 2 or 2* significance. These are some of the most important:

> The Bishop's Palace, a grand medieval series of buildings largely destroyed by the Parliamentarians during the Civil War. Standing on the south side of the Cathedral it is an manifestation of the power and wealth of Lincoln's medieval bishops.
>
> The Chancellory, on Priorygate opposite the Cathedral, is easily recognised by the grand oriel window on the first floor, it is believed to be Lincoln's oldest brick building.
>
> The Choristers House, stands near to Priory Gate Arch.

Built in 1661 it was converted into 3 residences in 1887

The Deanery, built by Dean, later Bishop, Gravesend in 1254. By the 19th century this building was in a poor state of repair and was replaced on the same site in the mid 1840s.

The Subdeanery stands to the south side of the Exchequer Gate. a medieval building, re-fronted in 1873 by J L Pearson . A mosaic and hypocaust was discovered on the site in the 18th century.

Cantilupe Chantry stands opposite the south east door of the Cathedral. Founded by Nicholas, Lord Cantilupe for a college of priests, to say mass for the souls of the founder and his relations at an altar.

The Vicars' Court, the entrance is on Greestone Lane, above the stairs. It was built as a 'college' for 20 Vicars Choral[1]. It was originally formed into a quadrangle but many of the other buildings have been removed, Thought to have been erected during the reign of Edward I, but much altered since.

The Vicars' Stables or Tithe Barn stands below the Vicars' Court and is a long two storey building built by

The Tithe Barn

Bishop Alnwick and John Breton in the 1440s. Lately used for storage and as a dining hall for the former Girls' High School on Lindum Road

In medieval times the most important people of the Cathedral were the Canons. often living elsewhere they appointed so-called 'Vicars Choral' to deputise for them.

20 MR SHUTTLEWORTH AND HIS HALL

The Lincoln Waterworks Company was established in 1846 to provide fresh drinking water to the growing city of Lincoln. One of the main requirements. of a fresh water system is a reservoir: Prial Drain gave a regular supply of fresh water so the Company built a dam at the north end adjacent to the road to Skellingthorpe.

The lake covered 25 acres and held 23 million gallons of water. The water was piped to the Boultham filter beds near Altham Terrace and then pumped to a service reservoir in Lincoln. The lake supplied a total of 733 homes and was used until 1911. It was long thought that the Skellingthorpe lake was responsible for the Lincoln Typhoid outbreak of 1905 but it is no longer thought to be the cause.

Joseph Shuttleworth was a successful engineer and a partner in Clayton Shuttleworth & Company needed a home suitable to his status. In 1861 he bought the lake and grounds, in 1862 Hartsholme Hall, designed by Major F H Goddard, was built for him. As well as the grand Hall with its stable block, cottages, laundry, battery house, farmstead; lodges on Skellingthorpe Road and Doddington Road were also constructed. The interior of the Hall took a further 2 years to complete.

The grounds were laid out by Edward Milner, the Victorian landscape gardener.

The Doddington Road Lodge was built in 1879 and the size of the estate was increased to about 300 acres. The boathouse was built in 1881. A gasworks for the Hall and buildings was installed, possibly by JTB Porter & Co of Lincoln who made many country house installations throughout England.

Joseph died in 1883, and his widow moved to Heighington Hall. The Hall passed to his eldest son, Alfred. Alfred lived mainly in The Close in Lincoln, later extending Eastgate House, now part of the Lincoln Hotel . Nathaniel Clayton Cockburn moved into the Hall in the mid 1890s.

In 1902 it was sold to Colonel Thomas Harding. Harding installed electricity in the Hall and re-erected a monument originally erected by the waterworks company to commemorate the building of the reservoir.

Lord Liverpool (Sir Arthur William de Brito Savile Foljambe (1870-1941)) bought the estate in 1909 for £16,250. Lord Liverpool was appointed Governor of New Zealand in 1912 and became the first Governor-General in 1917, retiring in 1920. He died at Canwick Hall in 1941.

The estate was sold to Thomas Place in 1939, but he never took up residence. The estate was requisitioned by the Army in 1942 for military training: the Hall was an officers mess.

At the end of hostilies the Hall was used used by homeless families, by 1947 32 families were squatting in it. Thomas Place put the estate up for sale and demanded compensation from Lincoln Corporation.

The Hall and 130 acres were sold to Lincoln Corporation,

the sale was eventually completed in 1951. The Hall was to be converted to an old peoples home but the neglect and damage sustained to the structure of the building meant that there was no alternative but to demolish it at a cost of £600.00. The kitchen block and other buildings were left standing for Civil Defence use. The kitchen block was eventually demolished in 1964.

Today Hartsholme Country Park is enjoyed by thousands of local people each year, unfortunately money is not available to restore the gardens to their former grandeur

ABOUT THE AUTHOR

Phil Gresham was born in Lincoln shortly after World War II. He has always been interested in the history of his home city and, when he returned to live near Lincoln after 40 years of living in other parts of the country, he wanted to share the history with other people to make them aware of all that Lincoln has to offer.

Also by Phil Gresham:

- It's About Lincoln: Snippets of History

You can follow him on:

- Twitter: @itsaboutlincoln
- Facebook group: https://www.facebook.com/groups/itsaboutlincoln
- Facebook Page: https://www.facebook.com/ItsAboutLincoln

Read more about Lincoln at:
http://www.itsaboutlincoln.co.uk